D0513400

PETRONAS TOWERS

Cesar Pelli and Michael J. Crosbie

PETRONAS TOWERS

The architecture of high construction

Acknowledgements
This book represents the results of an intense international collaboration of many architects, designers, clients, engineers and consultants. Their contributions have made this project the world-renowned, award-winning project it has become. In particular, I must thank Fred Clarke, partner in charge of this project; Lawrence Ng, its Project Manager; and Jon Pickard, its Design Team Leader.

I would also like to thank those who have contributed specifically to this book. Mig Halpine secured a publisher, compiled project illustrations and back matter and oversaw the book's production. John Apicella's thorough knowledge of the project was a significant resource in compiling project documentation and editing captions. Mike Crosbie adeptly brought cohesion and understanding to each chapter with his suggestions and text.

I wish to express my gratitude to our Editor, Maggie Toy, for accepting to publish the book, and to Mariangela Palazzi-Williams, Senior Production Editor, for her efforts in bringing the book to fruition.

Cesar Pelli

Front Cover: Jeff Goldberg/Esto, View of towers' pinnacles looking east
Back Cover: Jeff Goldberg/Esto, View of towers in city skyline at sunrise
Frontispiece: J. Apicella/CP&A, Frontal views of tower tops, bustle tops and skybridge

Design and prepress: Artmedia Press, London

First published in Great Britain in 2001 by
WILEY-ACADEMY

A division of
JOHN WILEY & SONS
Baffins Lane
Chichester
West Sussex PO19 1UD

ISBN: 0-471-49547-6

Other Wiley Editorial Offices
New York • Weinheim • Brisbane • Singapore • Toronto

Printed and bound in Italy

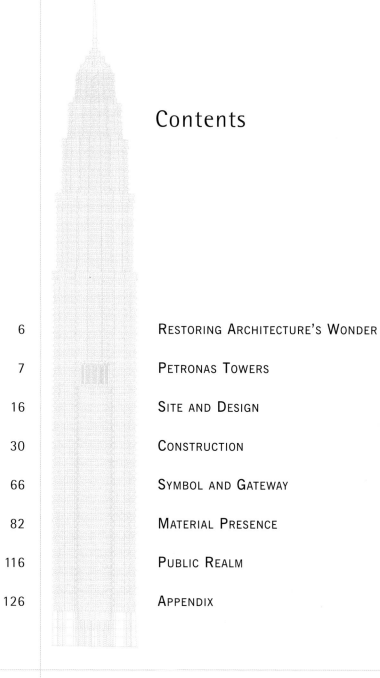

Contents

RESTORING ARCHITECTURE'S WONDER

A few years ago, architecture suffered a cultural setback that received little notice in architectural circles. A news magazine in the U.S. carried a cover story on the seven wonders of today. And on this list, there was not a single building. From ancient times, at least one work of architecture had always been among the world's wonders. Among the Seven Wonders of the Ancient World, one could count five buildings: the Pyramids of Egypt, the Hanging Gardens of Babylon, the Temple of Artemis at Ephesus, the Mausoleum at Halicarnassus, and the Pharos of Alexandria. But in a world with jumbo jets, microchips, and artificial hearts, architecture appears to have lost its wonder.

The Petronas Towers in Kuala Lumpur, now the tallest buildings on earth, rightfully restore architecture as a world wonder. Their design by Cesar Pelli reflects a melding of East and West. From the West, the Petronas Towers embody the great spirit of buildings that reach to the heavens, a spirit born on the plains of the American Midwest and now found on nearly every continent on earth. The towers reflect the latest technology in making tall buildings, with modern materials such as stainless steel cladding, which makes these spires glisten on the skyline.

From the East, Pelli's design embraces the architecture and decorative arts of Malaysia. When viewed in plan, the towers appear as two overlapping squares—interlocking heaven and earth—to create an eight-pointed star, which is further refined with half-circles between the star points. The spirit of the geometry is Islamic—the dominant Malaysian culture—and the geometric pattern is found throughout the country in screens, architectural ornament, and decorative arts.

Other Eastern cultural and environmental elements are woven into the towers' form. The conical spires which step back six times as they rise on the city skyline suggest ceremonial towers. The windows on the towers are shaded with deep overhangs, which help cut solar gain and cool this building in its tropical climate.

For Pelli, one of the towers' most significant architectural characteristics is Eastern in nature: the space between them. The Petronas Towers are placed on a central axis, framing a doorway to the infinite with a bridge that connects the two towers at the 41st and 42nd floors. In the spirit of Lao Tse, the Chinese philosopher who stressed that architecture's power lies not in its physical walls but instead in the space created by those walls, the towers together create a powerful super-scaled portal.

With the Petronas Towers, Pelli has created a truly "global" architecture. They open like the eye of a needle to thread the world, stitching two cultures together, and stand as a world wonder that joins East and West.

Michael J. Crosbie

PETRONAS TOWERS

THE BACKGROUND

In the early 1980s, the Malaysian government decided to relocate the Selangor Turf Club to the edge of the city. This presented the opportunity to develop this land to meet the demands of urban growth. The site is very well located in the heart of the commercial district, the Golden Triangle.

The Petronas Towers were planned as part of a larger complex, Kuala Lumpur City Centre. The client group, Kuala Lumpur City Centre Bhd., was created specifically to acquire and develop the 100-acre site previously occupied by the Selangor Turf Club. There is both private and public involvement in the project. Petronas, the national petroleum company of Malaysia, is both a part owner and a key tenant. Datuk Seri Dr. Mohathir Mohamad, the Prime Minister of Malaysia, has shown great interest in the design and construction progress of the buildings as part of "Wawasan (Vision) 2020," the government plan for Malaysian progress.

An international competition was held in 1990 to select a master plan for the site. The winning scheme was prepared by Klages, Carter, Vail and Partners of Costa Mesa, California. The city mayor and his planning team, KLCCB and its consultants made further improvements to the master plan, and it was later approved by the city planning authority.

THE DESIGN COMPETITION

The design of the Petronas Towers began, as most large-scale projects do today, with an international design competition. Representatives of the client interviewed over twenty international architects and visited many of their buildings. Eight firms from Asia, Europe and the United States were selected in June 1991 to participate in an invited competition. All architects worked with a relatively short brief that described project requirements and objectives. The designs were required to follow the Klages, Carter, Vail and Partners master plan. The entire 100-acre site of the Selangor Turf Club had been planned as a large development with a 40-acre public park in its center to be surrounded by privately developed office and apartment buildings and hotels.

Phase 1 in the northeast corner of the site was the subject of the competition. This corner has a prow form that juts into the center of the Golden Triangle, Kuala Lumpur's growing financial and commercial center. The architects were asked to provide a general design for a shopping center and public spaces, and a more detailed design for two towers to be occupied by Petronas, the national petroleum company of Malaysia. The Petronas Towers were expected to define a gateway into this new city center. The brief required that the design create "a place that people can identify as unique to Kuala Lumpur and Malaysia." During meetings with the client prior to the competition, their design intentions were made clearer: they wanted the towers to be Malaysian. That the towers should become the tallest buildings in the world was never discussed, only that they be beautiful and could become new symbols of the growing importance of the Petronas Company and the city of Kuala Lumpur.

The time allowed for the competition was brief. In a few weeks, the competitors had to understand the problem, develop good working solutions, make them into beautiful, or at least interesting buildings, and prepare measured drawings, rendered perspectives and models to send to Kuala Lumpur. The client's technical staff took two weeks to review all proposals, and in August 1991 all competitors were requested personally to present their designs and explain their intentions; first to a technical committee and on the following day to the Prime Minister Datuk Seri Dr. Mohathir Mohamad and to the principals of Kuala Lumpur City Centre Holdings Sdn. Berhad, the clients. During the presentations, the competitors had to answer technical and economic questions one day and aesthetic and philosophical ones the next.

Later in the month of August, my firm, Cesar Pelli & Associates, was selected to design the first phase of Kuala Lumpur City Center including the Petronas Towers. One never knows with certainty why one project is selected ahead of others. In this case, the impression given by the client was that our design answered all their pragmatic concerns with a well-resolved scheme and, most importantly, that it was the only one that proposed an image which they considered well suited to Malaysia.

Kuala Lumpur had experienced much growth in the previous fifteen years and many high-rise buildings had been constructed in its center. However, these buildings were perceived as unrepresentative of the climate and cultural traditions of Malaysia. Because of this, the client was very interested in an appropriate image for the whole design but was focused on two tall buildings. The design of tall buildings is very demanding. The taller the building, the greater the pragmatic requirements of function, structure, efficiency, and economy. Architectural expression is dependent on the intelligent resolution of many technical problems. The design of the Petronas Towers also required rethinking the character of tall buildings to free them from American and northwestern European associations and make them belong to Kuala Lumpur and Malaysia.

Perhaps the most important artistic decision we made was to design the towers as skyscrapers with distinctive silhouettes and to make the pair a single form. In the Modern Movement, architects have endeavored to pair buildings in asymmetric compositions, breaking all tension between them. It is usually preferred to make the two buildings of different heights (as most of the other competitors did) or, if the same height, to organise them diagonally to each other. The model for this approach is Mies van der Rohe's Lake Shore Drive towers, a beautiful pair of buildings. Mies's intention was to create abstract sculptural objects sitting on an empty plane and to avoid symbolic expression. These buildings correctly express the tenets of International Modernism and were the model used by Minoru Yamasaki in his design for the World Trade Center Towers in downtown Manhattan.

I have come to believe that International Modernism, due to the historical circumstances of its early development, never came fully to understand the problem of very tall buildings. The design of the Petronas Towers is an attempt to look at one aspect of the very tall building with fresh eyes, and to bring back to them essential qualities that were lost in the triumph of International Modernism. The Petronas Towers are not only symmetric in themselves, but they also create a distinctively shaped symmetric space between them. This space is the key element in the composition. Each tower has its own vertical axis; but, more importantly, the space between them also has a recognisable and memorable form. The center of the composition—the *axis mundi*—was transferred from the solid forms to the space they define. This central space is free of functions and the onlooker can assign spiritual or civic roles to it. We strengthened this quality by connecting the towers with a pedestrian bridge, not originally required by the clients. The bridge and the inclined struts that support it at its center create a 40-story-high portal to the sky. In many cultures, detached portals, or gates, represent thresholds to a higher world. This quality is evident in the sky portal in Kuala Lumpur.

The symbolic attribute resides in the space between the buildings. When I was in my initial year of architecture school at the University of Tucuman in Argentina, I was very impressed by my first encounter with a saying of Lao Tse that I remember as: "The reality of a vase is not in its clay walls but in the space they contain. The reality of a wheel is not in its spokes but in the space between them." I read this in a Spanish translation of a lecture Frank Lloyd Wright gave at the Chicago Art Institute in 1931. He had paraphrased an English version of the original ancient Chinese. The acorn of truth survived all the translations and remained within me for many years, to help me give form to the Petronas Towers and to make them unlike any Western skyscraper. Their qualities are not necessarily Malaysian (the country has no indigenous tradition of tall buildings), but as they appear for the first time in Kuala Lumpur, they will be forever identified with the place. In the same way the Eiffel Tower is identified with Paris, although its structure and form were not derived from Parisian or French architecture.

DEVELOPMENT OF THE DESIGN

The skybridge was not a requirement of the brief, but as the project developed it became an essential part of the overall functions of the towers. It links two sky lobby levels in both towers permitting easy access to meeting rooms, an executive dining room and a Surau (prayer room) distributed between the towers. Most interestingly, we discovered that by making the skybridge fire-rated and smoke-controlled, its mid-height location permits exiting from one tower to the other, as an alternative exit path. This reduces the cumulative demand in each tower and enabled us to avoid adding two fire stairs that would otherwise have been required from the sky lobbies down.

The structural design for the bridge was difficult because it had to accommodate possible differential movements of both buildings. The final solution was the simplest, clearest and most elegant. It is an inverted "V" shape three-pinned arch that supports the bridge in the center, accommodating all movements while maintaining it equidistant from both towers.

We tried to make the design of the Petronas Towers belong to their region in many ways. The national religion of Malaysia is Islam and it permeates the culture. This led us to base the geometry of the towers on Islamic geometric traditions; geometric underlays to forms are much more important in Islamic countries than in the West and are perceived and appreciated by most people in their societies. In the competition, we proposed a twelve-pointed star plan because it made for a graceful building and an efficient floor plan. The geometry of the plan was one of the elements that interested the Prime Minister of Malaysia, Dr. Mohathir. During the competition presentation he suggested that perhaps there are other geometric forms that would be more representative of Islamic design. After being selected, we researched traditional Islamic patterns and it became apparent that the eight-sided star obtained by superimposing two rotated squares was the most commonly encountered base for Islamic designs. The appropriateness of the form was confirmed when the client sent us a drawing with Dr. Mohathir's suggestion of using two interlocked squares as the basis for the towers' plans.

Just two interlocking squares create an eight-pointed star, but an unsuitable floor plan. We studied many variations in model form and analysed their plans with their cores and structure, and finally proposed a form with eight semi-circles superimposed in the inner angles of the eight-pointed star creating a sixteen-lobed form.

Charles Thornton, the structural engineer for the project, developed a brilliant system for the towers. Each one is supported by a ring of sixteen cylindrical columns (of high-strength reinforced concrete) placed on the inner corners of the star-shaped plan. They form what Thornton calls a "soft tube." Because the columns are in the inside corners, they tend to disappear from one's core of vision and the occupants have the feeling of a continuous window on a columnless space.

The silhouette of the towers was refined many times. Now, as each tower ascends, it sets back six times. In the upper setbacks, the walls tilt gently towards the center completing the form and visually strengthening the central axis of the skyscraper. Most of the architects selected for the competition had substantial experience in the design of tall buildings. We all knew which forms could be resolved later into practical buildings. This allowed for the competition to have a short schedule. After we won and were awarded the commission in December 1991, a team of consultants was assembled that included the structural engineers, Thornton-Tomasetti; mechanical engineers, Flack & Kurtz; space planners, Studios Associates; associate architect, Adamson & Associates; landscape designers, Balmori Associates; and elevator consultant, Katz Drago Company. Malaysian associates were required in all disciplines. Sixteen firms collaborated in the design of this project, not an unusual number for large-scale under-takings.

Critical first efforts were concentrated on the resolution of structure and floor plate. Almost at the same time, the central core containing all vertical systems of elevators, stairs, mechanical, electrical and plumbing shafts and equipment and toilets began to be refined to make it as functional and efficient as possible. "Efficiency" in high-rise office buildings describes the ratio between usable and gross floor areas. The efficiency of a typical floor in the Petronas Towers is 76%, a good ratio for very tall buildings.

The cores of the Petronas Towers are very compact. To provide good elevator service in a small area, each shaft does "quadruple duty." The concept used could be described as two tall buildings stacked one over the other with an elevator lobby at the base of each building. The upper floor users take high-speed shuttle elevators to the sky lobbies where they change to other elevators. All elevators are double-deckers serving two floors at the same time. Visitors use cabs at one of two lobby floors, depending on odd or even floor destinations. The system sounds complex but it is sim-ple and obvious in use.

Early in the design, when the form of the towers was being refined, we started to detail their exterior, testing each element in drawings and study models. Not only aesthetic aspects were considered. In the sunscreen design, for example, we considered that the type of glass and the amount of glazing affect overall exterior appearance and views and comfort in the interior. We also took into account that they affect the build-ing's impact on the environment through diminished needs for office lighting, cooling loads, mechanical equipment sizes and annual operating costs. For all aspects of the design, tentative solutions were analysed, discussed with consultants and submitted to the client for approval. Numerous review cycles were required to confirm that the form the design was taking corresponded to our vision, served well all technical needs and that the plans could accommodate effectively the different departments of Petronas.

Through the design of this project we made over 2,000 study models at many differ-ent scales and levels of finish, including a four bay, three-story high full-size mock up of the exterior wall, built on the site with several alternative details and materials being considered. When the exterior wall started to take form, it appeared to us that the material that would best express its formal richness was stainless steel. We proposed this to our client who authorised us to proceed with this intention but, concerned about possible high costs, required that we also develop an alternate wall in aluminum. There were differences in the detailing of these two walls due primarily to the fact that aluminum is more ductile and can be extruded; therefore, large three-dimensional elements such as sunshades could be bent to follow the curved forms of the plan. Stainless steel instead had to be used primarily in broken or rolled sheet forms and the sunshades had to be built in straight segments.

The full-sized mock-up allowed us to compare both walls and analyse their technical and visual characteristics. We all preferred the stainless steel wall but, still uncertain about costs, the two systems were fully developed as alternatives for bidding contractors to price. When the bids came in, the cost of the stainless steel wall was only slightly more expensive than the aluminum and so it was chosen. Now that the buildings are built, the soft gleam of the stainless steel and its ability to turn from gray to blue to yellow, reflecting the changing natural light conditions, has dispelled all doubts that this was the right decision.

The multiple facets created by the stainless steel form of the towers and the sculpted horizontal articulations of the projecting louvers not only reflect the sunlight and shine like the facets of a crystal, but the complex play of light and shadow on them also gives the towers the clear feeling of belonging to the tropics.

The design of these buildings maintained the basic form and image we had given them in the competition but as it developed it also changed in many ways. The twelve-pointed star plan evolved into a sixteen-lobed form, and the towers acquired pinnacles. The pinnacles, together with increases in the program and in technical requirement (such as raised floors), made the towers grow from an original height of 380m in our competition design to reach 451.9m, becoming the tallest buildings in the world. The element that required much detailed design study was the top of the building—how the towers would meet the sky and the image that they would create. We had proposed a pointed but pinnacle-less top in the competition. As the design of the towers developed, we felt that these forms needed to come to a clearer resolution, with an ascending gesture. Our clients agreed with us but expressed their concern to have these tops feel Malaysian and not be derived from American skyscrapers or church steeples. The design process was one of trial and error as we experimented with many formal culminations of the tower form, being uncertain of when our design suited the cultural traditions of Malaysia. Some designs we abandoned for aesthetic reasons; other options were presented to the client for comments. After several months of design and many attempts, I felt we had reached the right solution. The present design was strongly recommended by us and accepted by both the client group and their consultants, who agreed that these latter forms reflected well their culture and tradition.

This extended design process permitted both the client and us to refine the forms until they became the most handsome and appropriate of all those considered.

The project continued to evolve even after design was almost completed. Late test borings indicated difficult underground conditions. To avoid this problem, Thornton and Tomasetti, our structural engineers, recommended that both towers be moved 60m (200 ft) to the southeast. This required redesign of access roads and the commercial area, but it also created room for a large formal garden as a forecourt for the Petronas Towers. Balmori Associates designed this garden with lineal fountains in the model of Islamic gardens such as El Generalife, in the Alhambra in Granada, but with tropical trees and flowers. The garden and its fountains are already extremely popular and much enjoyed by the people of Kuala Lumpur. The formal garden is the counterpart of the central park designed by Burle Marx of Rio de Janeiro. This is a friendly picturesque design with many public amenities.

An even later and also critical change was the decision by the Petronas company, made when the project was already under construction, to add a major concert hall to the project. This decision was made when the project was already under construction. Although difficult to fit in the design, we welcomed the inclusion of such a public cultural facility in the project. We worked with Kirkegaard and Associates, acousticians, and with Theater Projects Consultants, theater functions consultants. The 860-seat Dewan Filharmonik Petronas was tightly placed on a third level between the towers. The main entrance to the complex (between the two towers) and the center lobby were redesigned with two grand interior staircases to make them appropriate approaches to the concert hall.

The interior of the concert hall also responds to Malaysian cultural sensitivities. Its sightlines and acoustics were designed to accommodate a full western orchestra with chorus and organ, and also very delicate traditional Southeast Asian music and dance. Walls and balconies are almost all wood with a design of horizontal bars alternating with narrow open slots that allow changes behind them to alter the acoustic qualities of the hall. The domed ceiling of the hall looks solid, but it is acoustically transparent. Above this ceiling we have provided an open volume of air, almost as large as that of the concert hall itself. Movable baffles and acoustically absorbent panels make it possible to substantially alter the resonance qualities of the hall to accommodate its changing presentations.

In its final form, the first phase of the Kuala Lumpur City Centre development has a site area of 14.15 acres and more than 99,500m^2 (10,700,000 sq ft) of mixed-use development. The 88-story Petronas Towers have an area of 427,500m^2 (4,600,000 sq ft). There are 140,000m^2 (1,500,000 sq ft) of retail/entertainment facilities; 251,000m^2 (2,700,000 sq ft) of below-grade parking and service facilities for 5,000 cars; and two office towers with approximately 186,000m^2 (2,000,000 sq ft). One, designed by Kevin Roche, is already built. Public functions within the complex include an art gallery, the Dewan Filharmonik Petronas Concert Hall, a petroleum discovery center, and a multi-media conference center.

WHY SKYSCRAPERS?

Why do we build tall buildings? Very tall structures were built at great effort by almost every culture in all regions of the earth. The urge to build as high as possible appears to be a common trait of human culture. It is recorded in the Bible in the story of the Tower of Babel, "and they said: go to, let us build us a city and a tower whose top may reach unto heaven." The builders thought that they could reach heaven with their construction, and apparently so did God, and He punished them for their audacity. What interests me most in the biblical account is that its writers took it for granted that the human desire to build as high as possible was universally shared.

Ancient Egyptians started building pyramids some 5,000 years ago and the height of the Great Pyramid of Cheops in Gizeh (147m) was not surpassed by any building until the 19th century. Ziggurats in Mesopotamia are almost as old and were probably the model for the Tower of Babel. The steps of many ziggurats represented the seven levels of heaven and it was thought that the priests who climbed them reached the apex of the universe. These structures were basically piles of stone or brick, but to be very tall and vertical they required the most sophisticated engineering of the time. Mayan pyramids, Egyptian obelisks, Chinese pagodas, and Moslem minarets are examples of the widespread desire to build not only tall, but as thin as possible. All these structures strive to be taller than anything nearby. Their vertical forms were often seen against the horizon, or emerging above a horizontal line of trees or rooftops. They perhaps recreate the primeval image of a person standing against the horizon line, two intersecting lines, representing humanity and the earth.

Very tall structures are place markers. The steeple of Salisbury Cathedral (1258) is seen at a great distance, even today, as a thin, pointed, very tall gesture that marks a special place. Steeples of churches have marked towns all over Christendom and they are essential in the traditional image of a medieval city or a New England town. Today, the tallest structures in most cities are skyscrapers and they also mark urban places. Sometimes, they also give form to our cities; they are not monuments, but places of work, office buildings. Skyscrapers were made possible by the invention of the elevator by Elijah Otis in 1852, and the development of iron and then steel structures. The first skyscraper was either the Western Union Building by George Post (New York, 1875) or the Home Life Insurance Building by William LeBaron Jenney (Chicago, 1884), depending on the definition used. That ten-story-structures such as these would not be considered skyscrapers today points to a peculiar quality of this building type: its dependence on its relationship with its surroundings. The invention of the skyscraper and the development of practical and theoretical knowledge of its properties took place almost entirely in two American cities: Chicago and New York. Skyscrapers remain as preeminently American building forms although they are being built all over the world.

There were four main periods in the development of the skyscraper; the first began around 1880 and lasted until 1908–1909. During this period, architects tried to adapt existing building types, most notably the Renaissance *palazzo*, to the new heights allowed by elevators. The first "skyscraper" may have been built in New York, but it is in Chicago where the great buildings of this period were constructed or designed. The very high buildings of this era went no higher than 14 stories (much lower than the Great Pyramid of Cheops) and not one of them plays the role of skyscraper in today's context. The second period, when skyscrapers grew to full bloom, started in the early 20th century and was brought to a close by the Great Depression. This took place primarily in New York. The Metropolitan Life Insurance Company Tower by Napoleon Le Brun (New York, 1909) marks its beginning. Rather than the traditional *palazzo* form, the architect selected a tower as his model: the campanile in the Piazza San Marco in Venice. He did this because the tower-campanile expresses another important aspect of the skyscraper: the celebration of the ability to build a vertical object so tall that it becomes the dominant element on the skyline. The Chrysler and the Empire State Buildings, built in this period, are still seen by most people as best expressing the potential beauty of skyscrapers.

The third period started after World War II and lasted until the mid 1970s. Buildings were designed within the framework of International Modernism that had become the dominant direction in architecture. Mies van der Rohe was the most influential designer of tall buildings in this period. They were rectangular, prismatic forms with flat roofs. Because modernist buildings avoided symbolic qualities he called his tall buildings high-rises and not skyscrapers. The fourth period started in the late 1970s and is still developing. It has seen the internationalisation of skyscrapers and a renewed interest in their silhouettes and symbolic potential. The Petronas Towers are a good example of this latest period.

The towers reached their maximum height in March 1996 and started to be occupied in January 1997. The Dewan Filharmonik Petronas Hall hosted its first concert in August 1998 and the grand opening celebration for the Petronas Towers took place in August 1999. Since their forms started to emerge on the Kuala Lumpur skyline, the Petronas Towers have become familiar and important symbols of pride and achievement for the people of Kuala Lumpur and Malaysia. The towers appear again and again over the trees and rooftops of the city and their combined silhouette is instantly recognisable although always changing. I believe the Petronas Company, KLCC Berhad, and the people of Malaysia possess now, in our executed design, exactly the proud symbol they had hoped for.
Cesar Pelli

SITE AND DESIGN

The site for the Petronas Towers is the "Golden Triangle." Around it radiates the city of Kuala Lumpur, Malaysia's capital. The site is not only geographically central, but symbolically so. It has become the locus of the country's future, where a new vision of Malaysia is in formation. The towers are the centerpiece of that vision and of the site itself.

The jewel of this 100-acre site are the towers. Working within a mixed-used development master plan by the U.S. firm of Klages, Carter, Vail & Partners, Cesar Pelli's design appeared to capture all of the aspirations of Malaysia in its flight to the future. The design drawings show a complex of buildings growing from an intimate relationship with the site, generating from its core. At the heart of the design, between the two towers, Pelli located a concert hall that provides an important gathering space. To the northwest of the towers is a grand landscaped garden, providing just the right forecourt to Malaysia's gateway to the 21st century.

From ancient Islamic forms of eight-pointed stars and decorative motifs, Pelli elaborated and refined the towers' design. A sixteen-lobed perimeter tower wall suggests its Islamic roots without being literal, maximising the exterior wall surface around the tower core. Setting the towers back as they rise, Pelli accentuates their height. When viewed from below, the foreshortening propels the towers into the heavens.

OPPOSITE: Schematic design rendering by Lee Dunnette;
RIGHT: Cesar Pelli & Associates schematic design site model

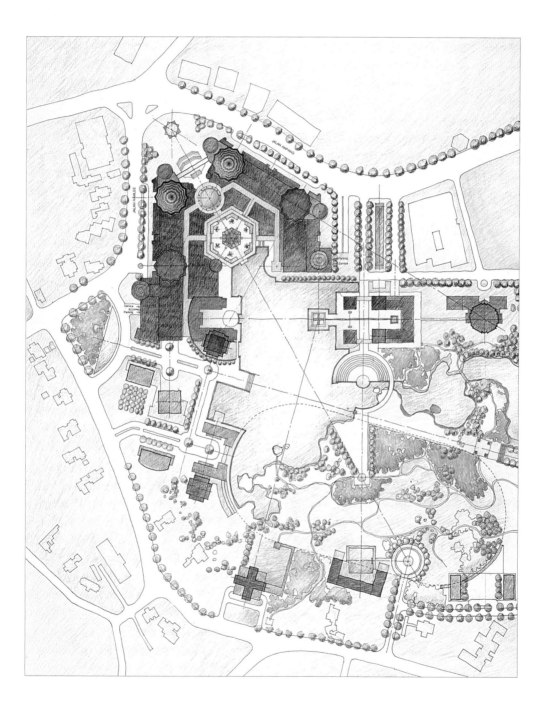

OPPOSITE: Competition site
plan; TOP: Competition base
podium level 2 plan; BOTTOM:
Competition base podium
below-grade level

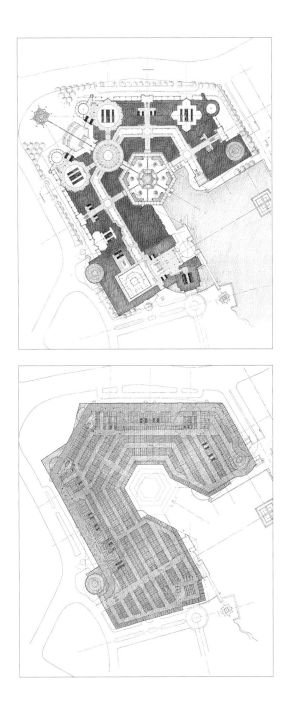

OPPOSITE: Master plan site
model photograph;
BELOW: Competition
concept sketch

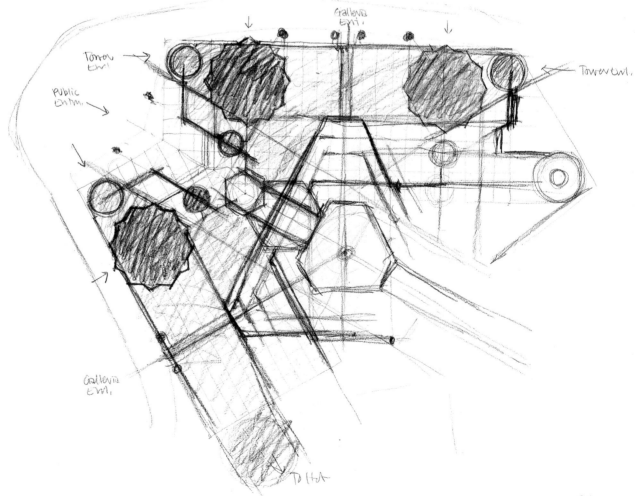

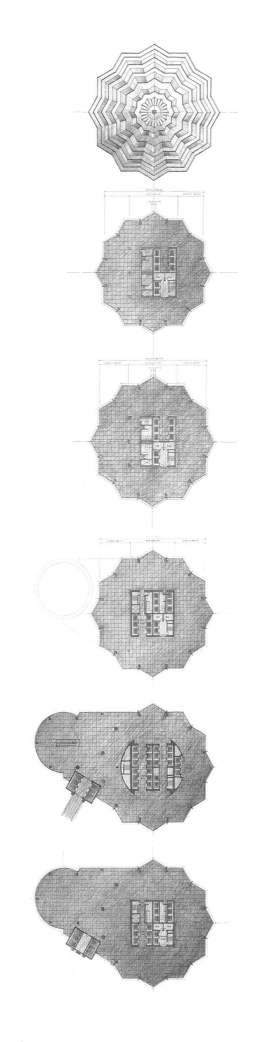

LEFT (from the top):
Roof plan,
typical plan levels 75-83;
typical plan levels 62-74;
typical plan levels 43-61;
typical plan level 38,
sky lobby;
typical plan levels 11-37;
OPPOSITE: Competition
model

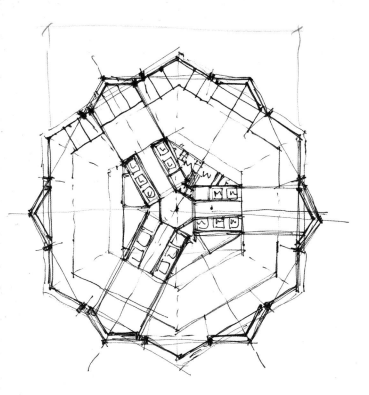

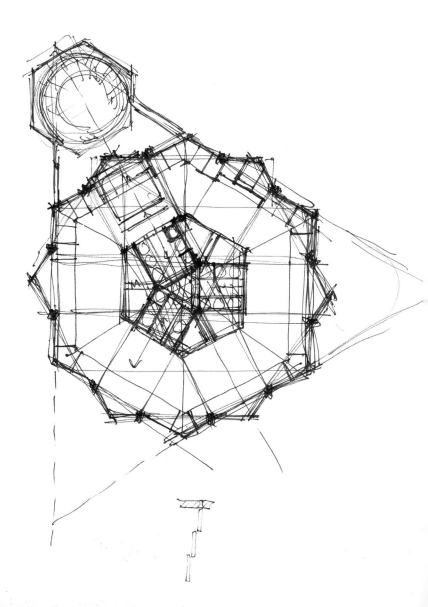

24

OPPOSITE: Competition conceptual tower plan studies;
RIGHT: Competition space planning options for typical office level

ABOVE: Competition northwest building elevation; OPPOSITE: Competition structural concepts

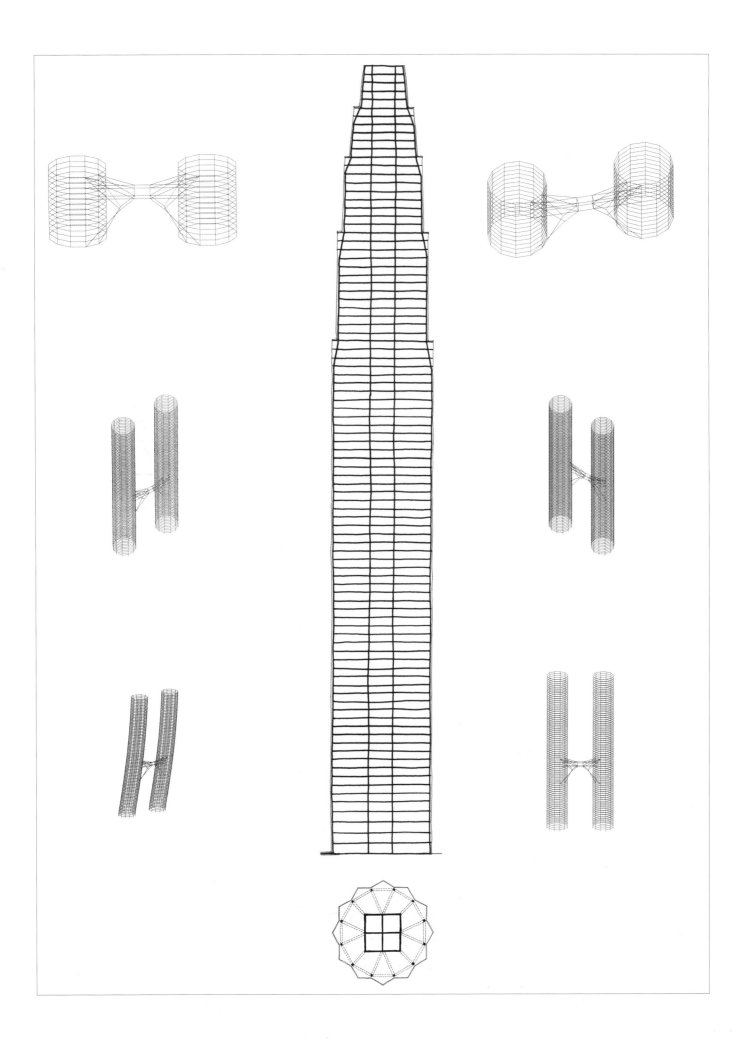

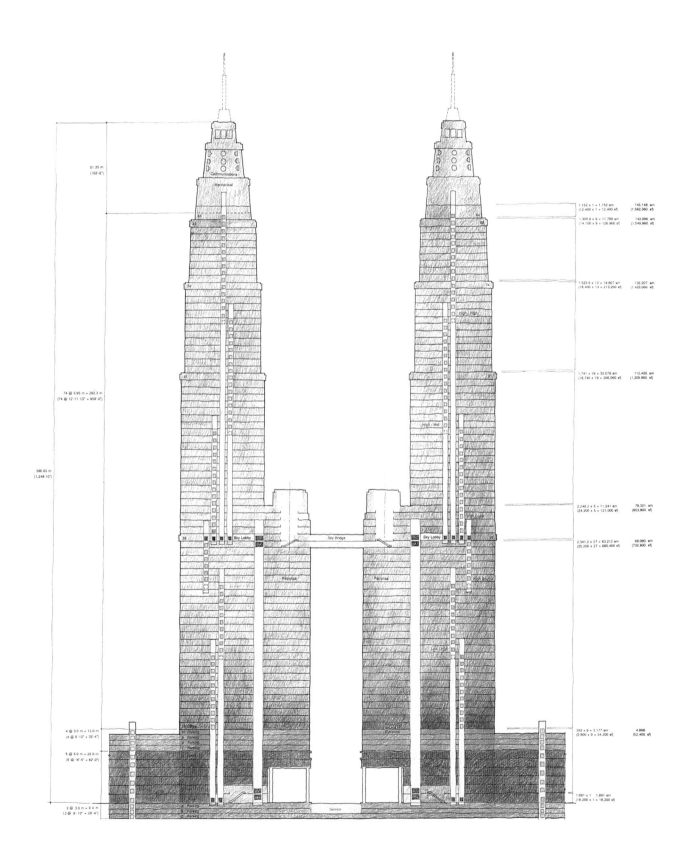

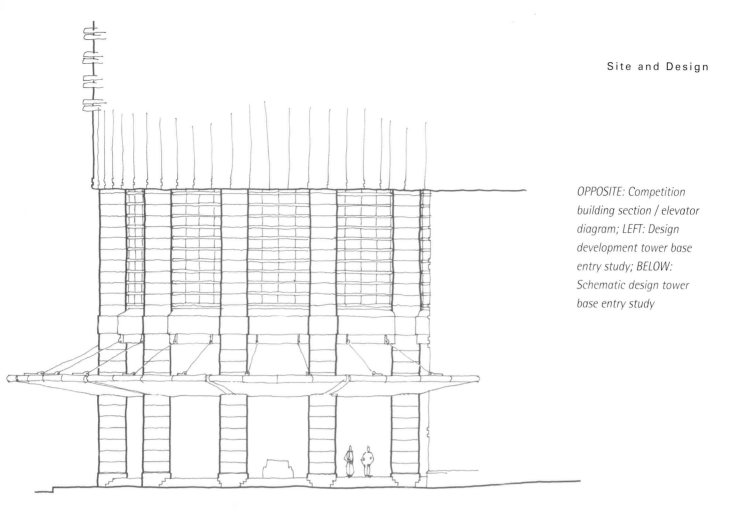

OPPOSITE: Competition building section / elevator diagram; LEFT: Design development tower base entry study; BELOW: Schematic design tower base entry study

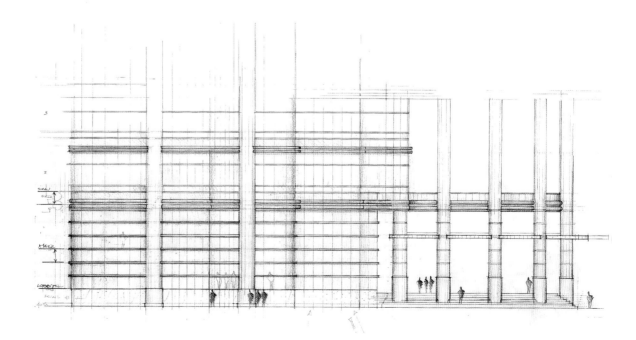

CONSTRUCTION

One of the first challenges of construction was anchoring the towers to the ground. The bedrock beneath the site was feared to be very irregular and Thornton-Tomasetti, the structural engineers, suggested relocating the towers about 200 feet so that they could bear on soil. The solution was to use an underground forest of friction piles which would provide greater distribution of the towers' weight. Over the piles was poured a reinforced concrete foundation mat, upon which the towers rest.

The towers are framed with a structure of concrete core walls and columns which, according to the engineers, was the best choice for several reasons. In Malaysia, the local contractors on the job were more familiar and comfortable working with concrete than with steel. Concrete also provided better stability to dampen the sway of the towers in winds, and minimised vibration.

Construction of the towers was fast-paced, thanks in part to the decision to let two contracts, one for each tower, to two separate contractors. This naturally created a competitive environment, to the benefit of the building. One of the most dramatic feats was the placement of the two-story skybridge, which was built on the ground and hoisted to its location joining the 41st and 42nd floors. After it was lifted into position, the legs which had been installed on the towers were swung down into place, and connected under the bridge.

OPPOSITE: Construction photograph tower 1 and 2, January 1995; ABOVE: Design development curtainwall section detail study; RIGHT: Raising of skybridge, August 1995

31

ABOVE LEFT: *Early tower foundation construction, January–February 1994;*
ABOVE RIGHT: *Early tower foundation construction, January–February 1994;*
MIDDLE: *Early tower foundation construction, January–February 1994;*
BELOW: *Project site geometry and orientation study showing north and Kibla (facing Mecca)*

OPPOSITE TOP: *Tower structure location diagram;*
OPPOSITE BOTTOM: *Early tower foundation construction, January–February 1994*

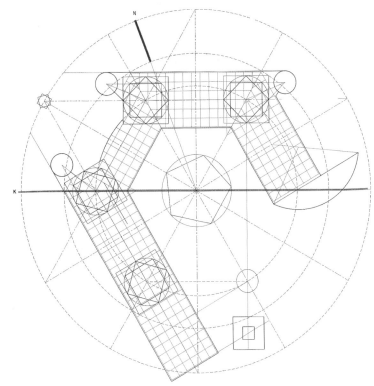

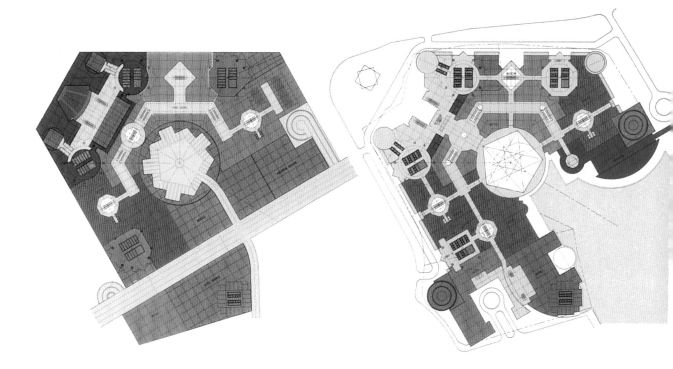

ABOVE LEFT: Master plan base podium stacking study, concourse level; ABOVE RIGHT: Master plan base podium stacking study, street level; FAR LEFT: Pouring concrete for towers foundation mat; LEFT: 14ft concrete tower foundation mat

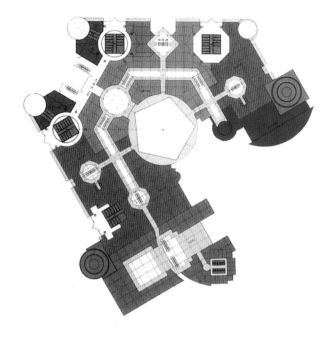

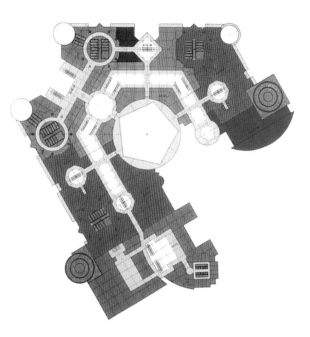

ABOVE LEFT: Master plan
base podium stacking study,
level 2; ABOVE RIGHT:
Master plan base podium
stacking study, level 3; LEFT:
Column form work rising
out of foundation mat,
March 1994

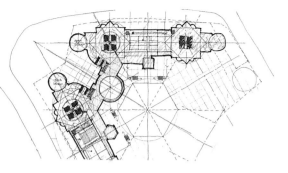

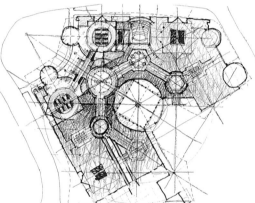

LEFT: Tower core and columns rising above foundation mat, May 1994; RIGHT: Tower core and columns rising above foundation mat–detail, May 1994; ABOVE AND BELOW: Conceptual base podium stacking studies

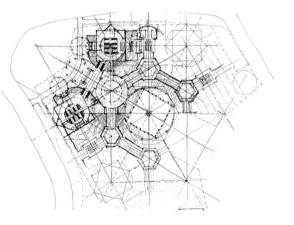

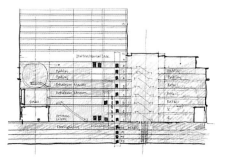

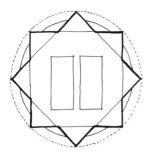

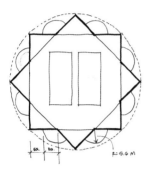

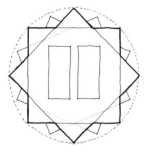

*LEFT: Master plan
floorplate studies;
BELOW: Tower columns at
street level lobby*

Petronas Towers

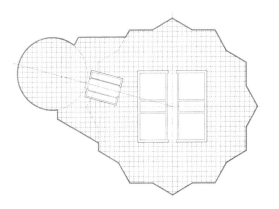
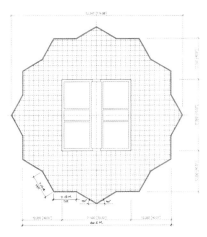
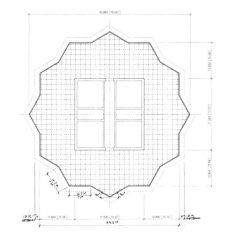

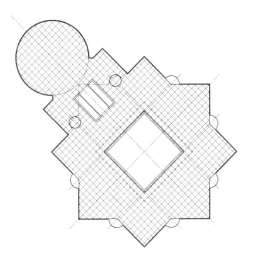

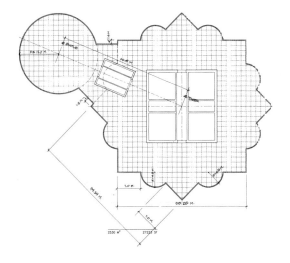

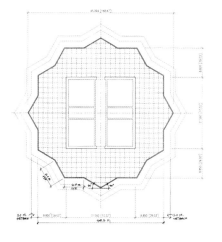

OPPOSITE: Early on-site curtainwall mock-up; OPPOSITE AND BELOW: Master plan floorplate studies

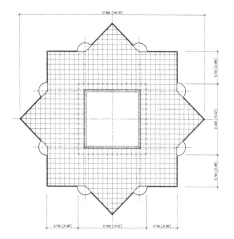

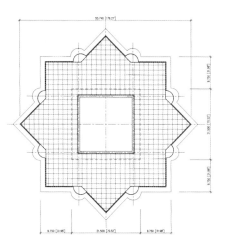

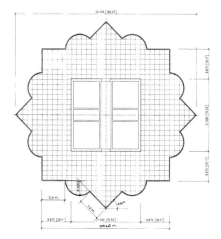

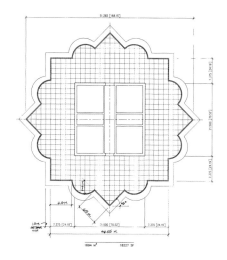

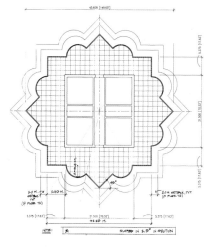

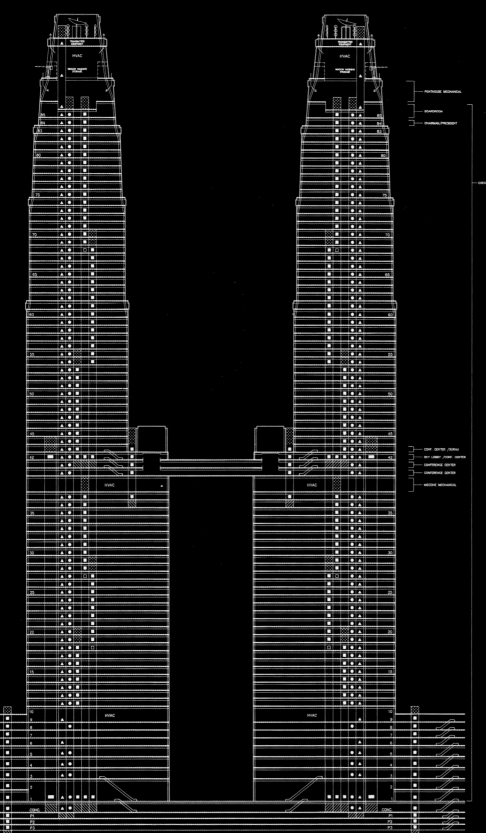

LEFT: Master plan elevator diagram; OPPOSITE: View of tower base podium construction and curtainwall installation

LEFT: Early tower curtainwall installation; OPPOSITE: Tower construction looking northeast, May 1995

BELOW: Early Design
development street level
main entrance
elevation; OPPOSITE:
Tower construction looking
northeast, May 1995

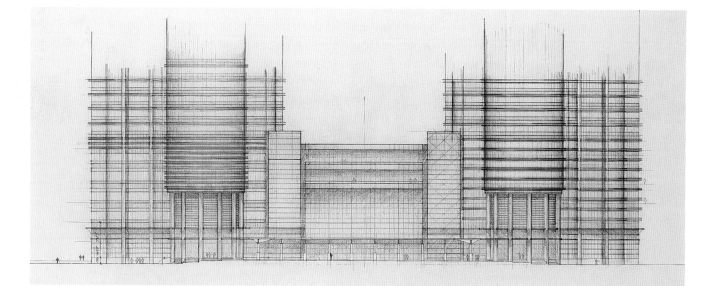

OPPOSITE: Detail of cantilevered steel floor structures for projecting bays; ABOVE: Studies of projecting set-back floor curtainwall; RIGHT: Steel floor framing and concrete superstructure

Petronas Towers

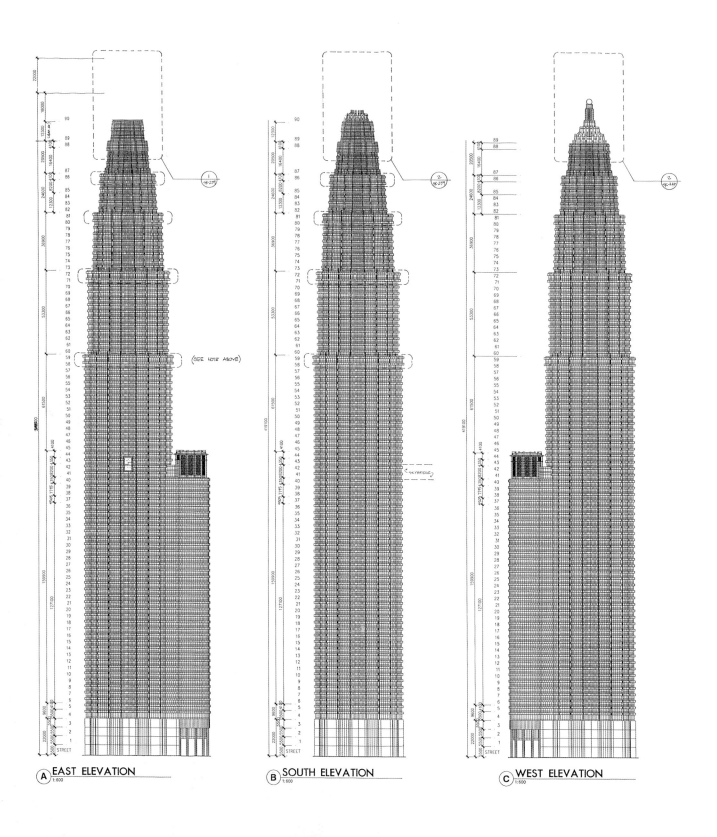

(A) EAST ELEVATION
1:600

(B) SOUTH ELEVATION
1:600

(C) WEST ELEVATION
1:600

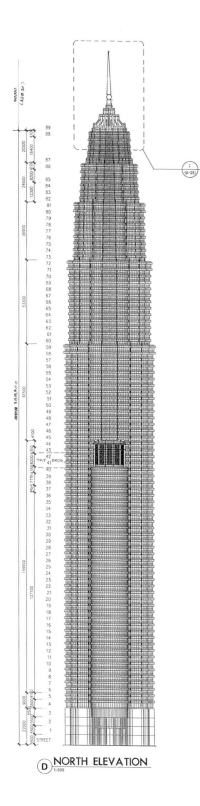

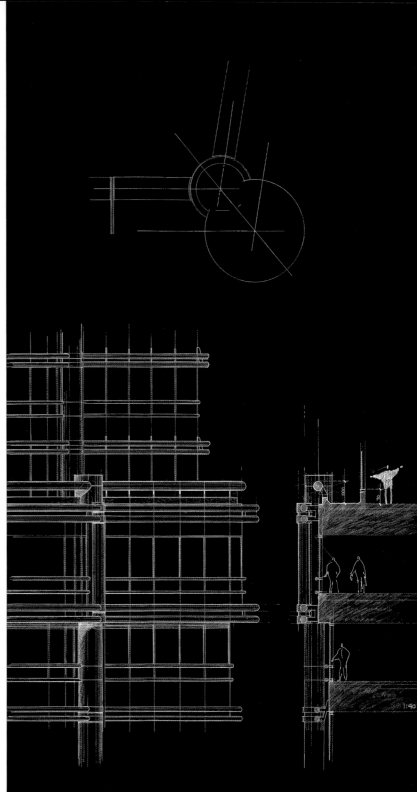

LEFT: Tower elevations showing alternative tower tops; ABOVE: Projecting set-back floor curtainwall elevation study

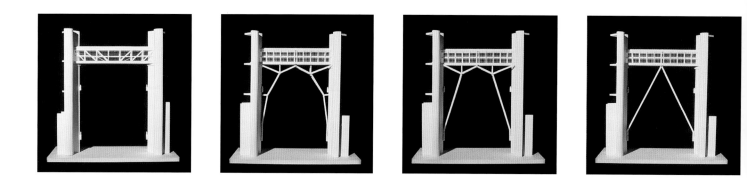

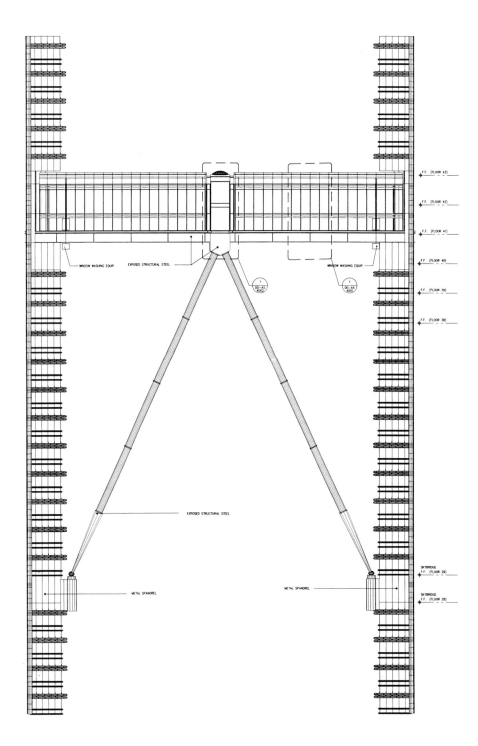

WINDOW WASHING EQUIP.

EXPOSED STRUCTURAL STEEL

WINDOW WASHING EQUIP.

F.F. (FLOOR 43)

F.F. (FLOOR 42)

F.F. (FLOOR 41)

F.F. (FLOOR 40)

F.F. (FLOOR 39)

F.F. (FLOOR 38)

1
DD-A5
400

1
DD-A5
400

EXPOSED STRUCTURAL STEEL

METAL SPANDREL

METAL SPANDREL

SKYBRIDGE
F.F. (FLOOR 29)

SKYBRIDGE
F.F. (FLOOR 28)

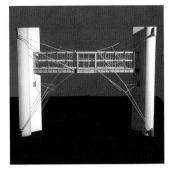

OPPOSITE TOP:
Skybridge study models;
OPPOSITE BOTTOM:
Skybridge elevation;
ABOVE LEFT: Early
structural skybridge model;
ABOVE RIGHT: Detail of
final skybridge model;
RIGHT: Elevation of
skybridge shortly after
final structural assembly

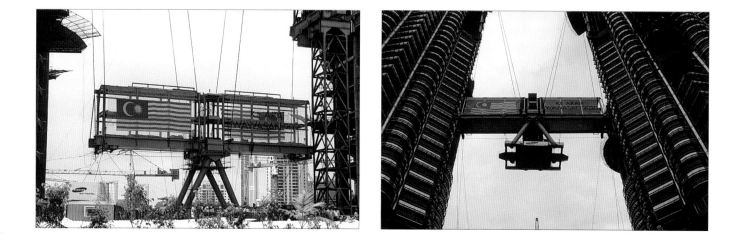

ABOVE LEFT: Skybridge at
ground level during raising
ceremony; ABOVE RIGHT:
Skybridge being raised into
place; OPPOSITE TOP:
Skybridge approaching leg
supports; OPPOSITE BOTTOM:
Construction details of skybridge leg supports

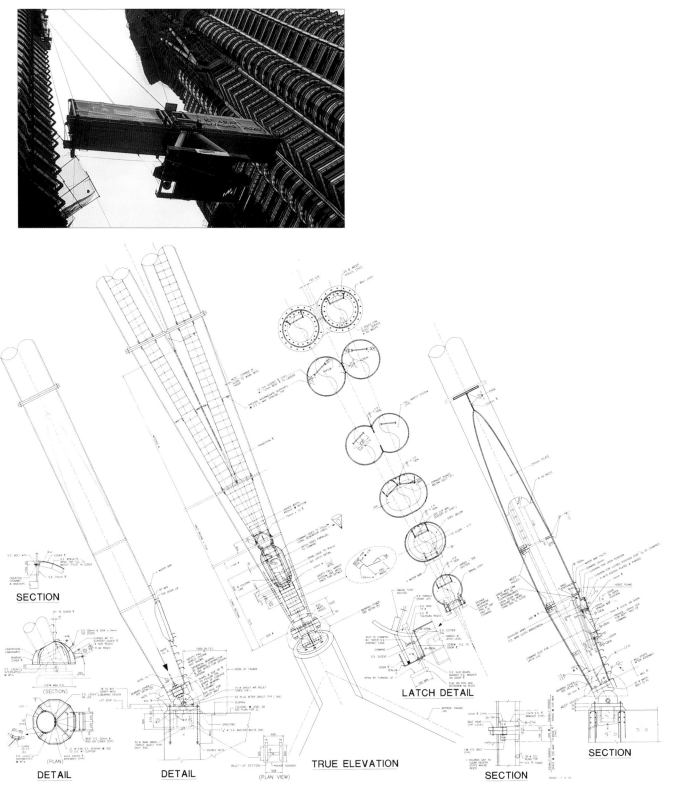

SECTION

DETAIL

DETAIL

TRUE ELEVATION

LATCH DETAIL

SECTION

SECTION

Petronas Towers

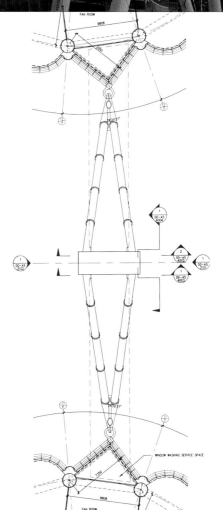

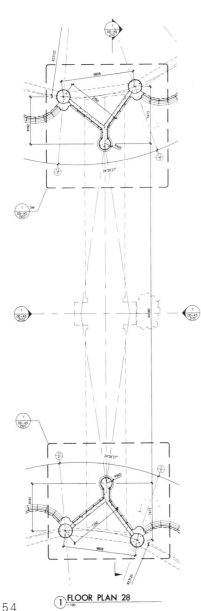

EXPOSED STRUCTURE

① FLOOR PLAN 28
1:100

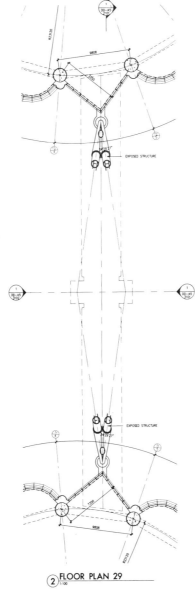

FAN ROOM

EXPOSED STRUCTURE

WINDOW WASHING SERVICE SPACE

FAN ROOM

② FLOOR PLAN 29
1:100

③ FLOOR PLAN 40
1:100

OPPOSITE TOP: Final assemblage of skybridge in place at levels 41 and 42; OPPOSITE BOTTOM: Plans of skybridge legs and leg supports; BELOW: Reflected ceiling plans of skybridge

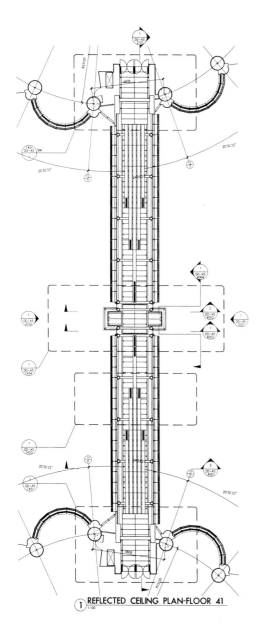

① REFLECTED CEILING PLAN-FLOOR 41
1:100

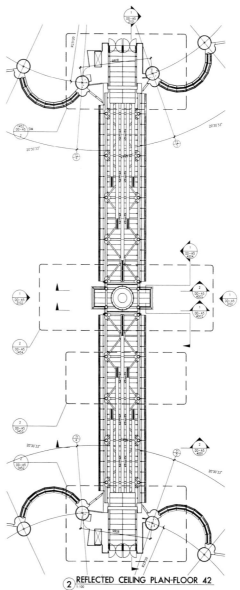

② REFLECTED CEILING PLAN-FLOOR 42
1:100

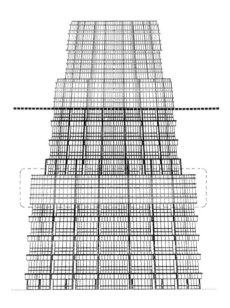

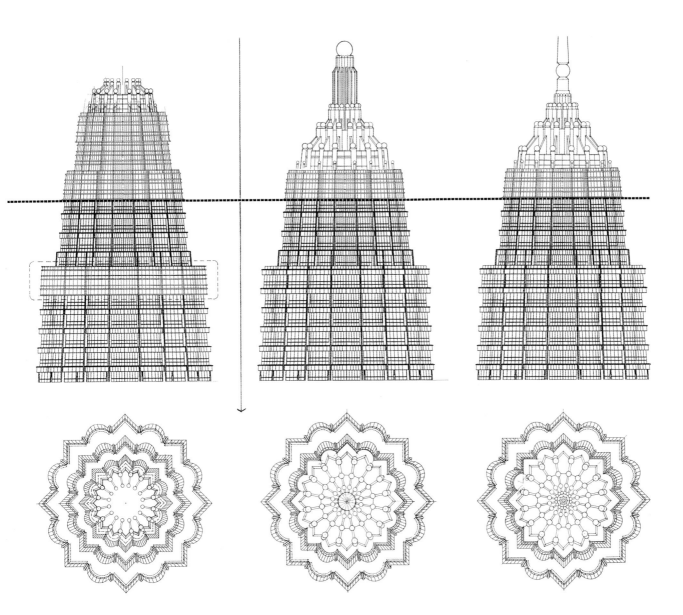

ABOVE: Alternative tower tops; OPPOSITE: Tower top model studies

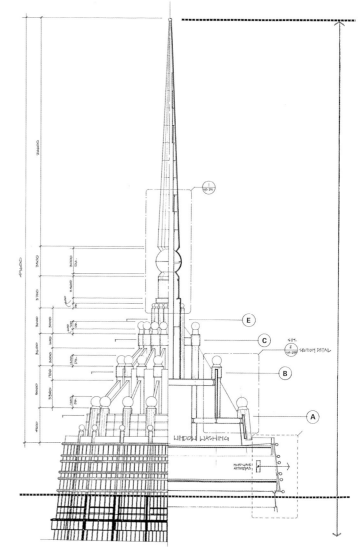

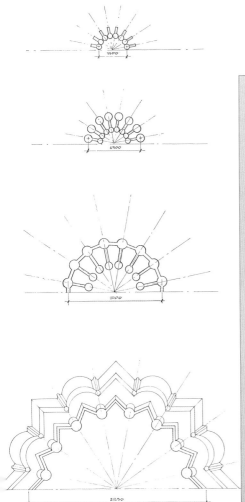

OPPOSITE LEFT: Final positioning of tower pinnacle, March 1996; OPPOSITE RIGHT: Pinnacle elevation/section study; ABOVE: Studies of concentric pinnacle geometry; RIGHT: Construction photograph from below of ring ball and pinnacle, March 1996

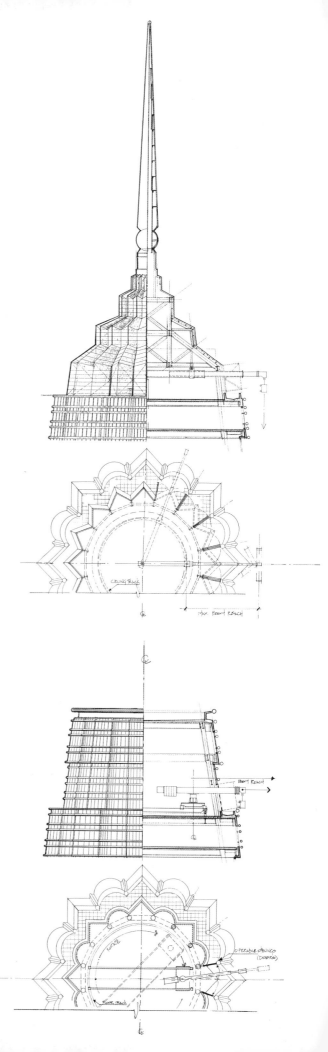

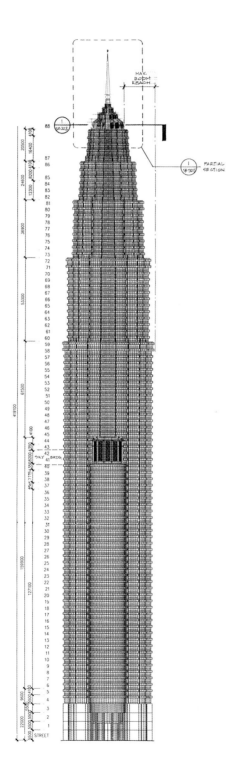

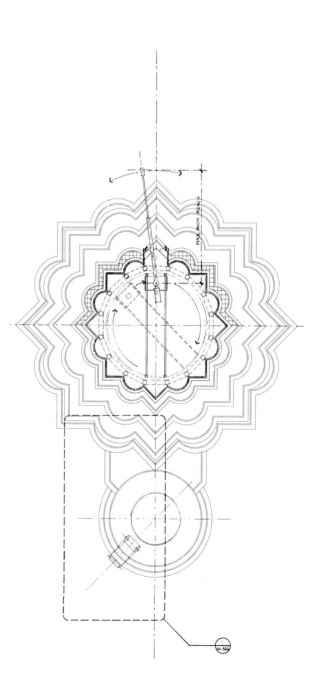

OPPOSITE: View of tower construction from west, June 1996; BELOW LEFT: North tower elevation; BELOW RIGHT: Plan through pinnacle showing extension and rotation of window washing boom

Construction

*ABOVE: View of towers in
city skyline from
northwest, June 1996;
OPPOSITE: Detail of
pinnacle stainless steel
cladding, September 1996*

SYMBOL AND GATEWAY

Traditionally, architecture has served as a symbol of power, a signifier of accomplishment, and the Petronas Towers continue this tradition. Pelli has written extensively about the power of the skyscraper to mark a geographic and symbolic place, and the competition jury that selected his design for Petronas seems to have understood this. There are many ways of providing space for work, space for shopping, for dining, and settings for civic life. But Pelli has satisfied these programmatic needs with a structure whose design is strong enough also to bear the weight of national and cultural aspirations.

On the Kuala Lumpur skyline, the towers seem to fulfill the goal stated in the project brief, that the design create a place unique to Malaysia. With spires reaching into the clouds, the towers celebrate the role of this country in the new world economy. Two towers not only suggest Malaysia's ability to straddle the cultures of East and West, but also offer the opportunity to create a gateway between them —a portal into Malaysia, and out to the rest of the world.

If today's skyscrapers are indeed our contemporary cathedrals, then within the history of tall buildings Petronas stand as the Chartres of skyscrapers—tall not only in their physical dimension, but the apex of our desire to join the earth to the heavens through architecture.

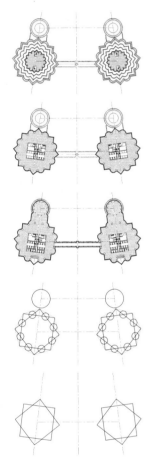

OPPOSITE: Night time view from south across the Kuala Lumpur City Centre (KLCC) Park designed by Roberto Burle Marx, September 1998;
ABOVE: Diagram of evolution of floor plate;
RIGHT: Night time view of skybridge

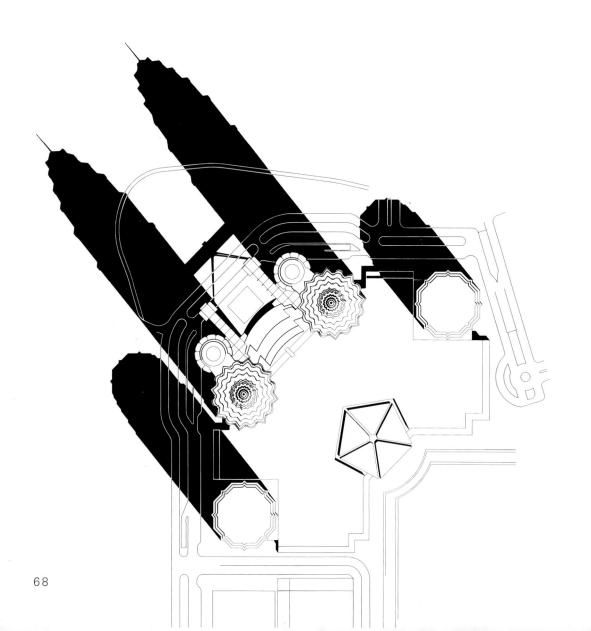

Kuala Lumpur.   C. Pelli '94

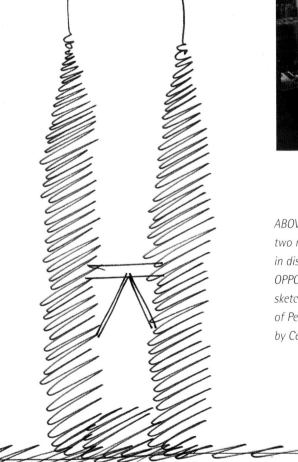

*ABOVE: View from tower
two ring ball with KL Tower
in distance;
OPPOSITE AND LEFT:
sketches of front elevation
of Petronas Towers
by Cesar Pelli*

*OPPOSITE: View
from northeast;
RIGHT: Detail of tower
top with window
washing boom at right*

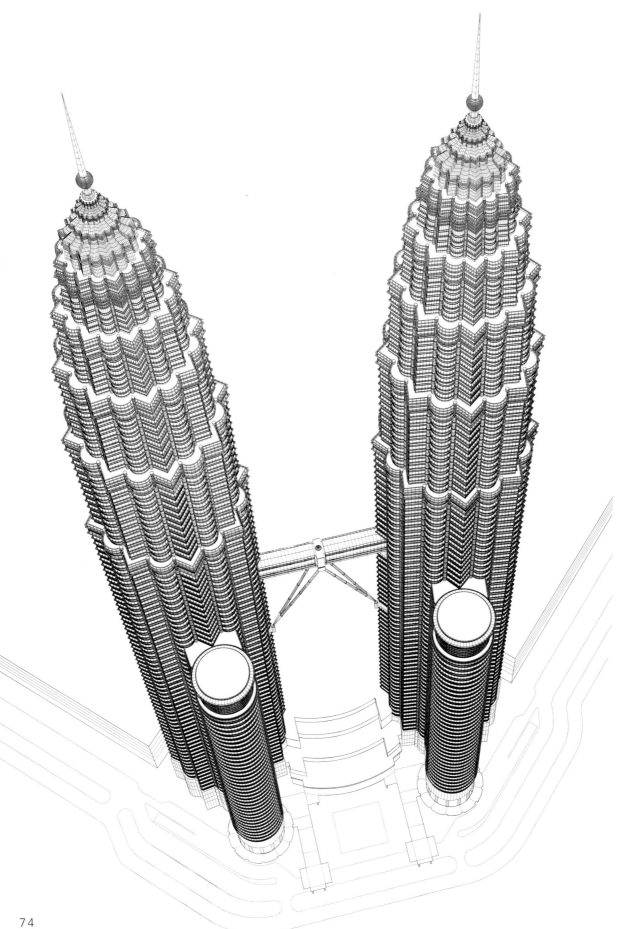

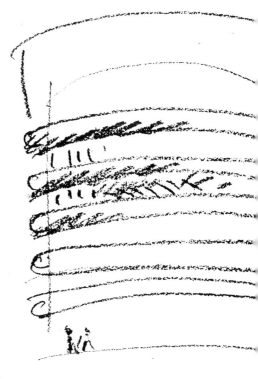

OPPOSITE: Bird's eye view;
ABOVE: View from
northeast;
RIGHT: Conceptual sketch
of bustle top

*OPPOSITE: View of towers
from Tun Razak;
ABOVE: View of towers
from Jalan Raja Chulan*

OPPOSITE: View southeast
of towers from city;
ABOVE: View of towers
rising above city from North
Klang Valley Expressway

OPPOSITE: Detail of Malaysian
architecture with towers on the
background;
RIGHT: View of towers at night
from Tasik Titiwangsa Lake;
BELOW: View of towers in city
skyline at sunrise

MATERIAL PRESENCE

One of the hallmarks of Cesar Pelli's architecture is its material presence. The choice of materials and finishes, the rendering of the building's surface under different qualities of light, the linking of interior and exterior treatments, and the expression of how a building is constructed are issues that are given careful consideration.

Petronas Towers reflect Pelli's particular attention to the buildings' skin. The stainless steel cladding shimmers in the Malaysian sun, alternating with ribbons of glass. Shading the windows are elegant stainless steel louvers whose tear-drop forms add another layer of articulation to the towers. Below the windows, framing the spandrel panels, are bullnose moldings also of stainless steel. As the stainless steel spire of the 70-year-old Chrysler Building in New York portends, the Petronas Towers will no doubt look as fresh and sparkling a century from now.

Inside the towers, materials and colors are rendered with a variety of patterns that are variations on geometric themes found in both Eastern and Western architecture—Islamic decoration meets the rose window of Christian tradition.

Pelli has observed that architecture can grow only if it is rooted in a living tradition of building construction. Petronas Towers reflect the material realities of building tall structures today, and how the architect can use them to give life and soul to architecture.

OPPOSITE and RIGHT: Night time view of opening ceremony celebrations from Petronas Plaza , August 1999

OPPOSITE: View from the tower two ring ball; RIGHT: View of the dramatic lighting of a tower top at night

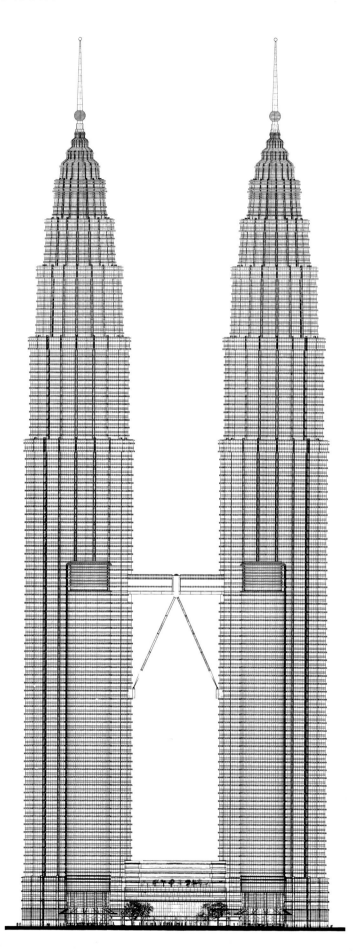

LEFT: Petronas Plaza and
ground level lobby plan;
BELOW: Paving plan of
tower one and two;
OPPOSITE: Detail of
entrance to towers and
concert hall

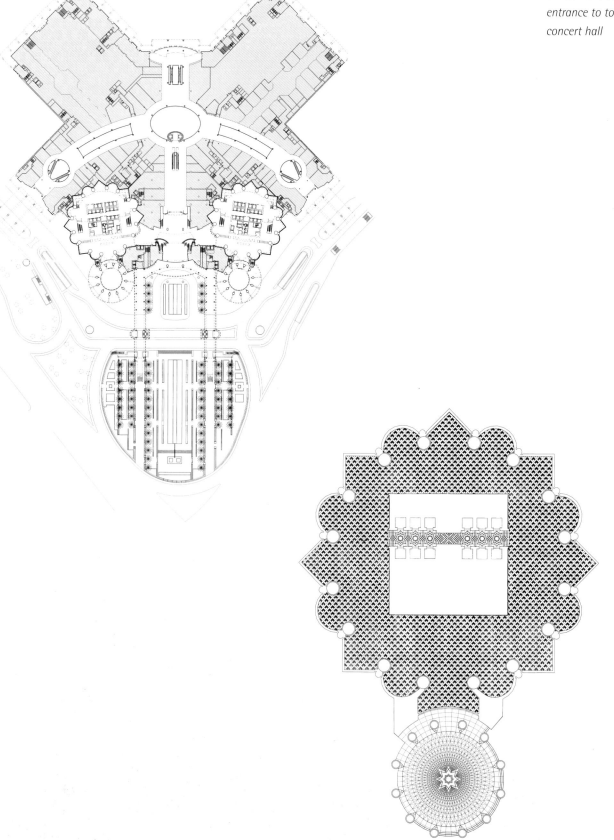

OPPOSITE TOP: Level 73, executive office conceptual layout; OPPOSITE BOTTOM: Level 40, conference center conceptual layout; RIGHT: View up tower showing sunshades and articulated curtainwall

OPPOSITE: Worm's eye
view; BELOW: Night time
view looking up to
skybridge

TOP: View up towers from Petronas Plaza;
MIDDLE: View up towers from forecourt;
BOTTOM: View of skybridge from top of adjacent building;
OPPOSITE TOP: Detail of observation area at skybridge mid-span;
OPPOSITE MIDDLE: Detailed perspective of skybridge;
OPPOSITE BOTTOM: Detail view of skybridge leg support and adjacent curtainwall

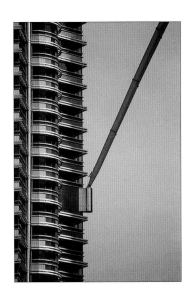

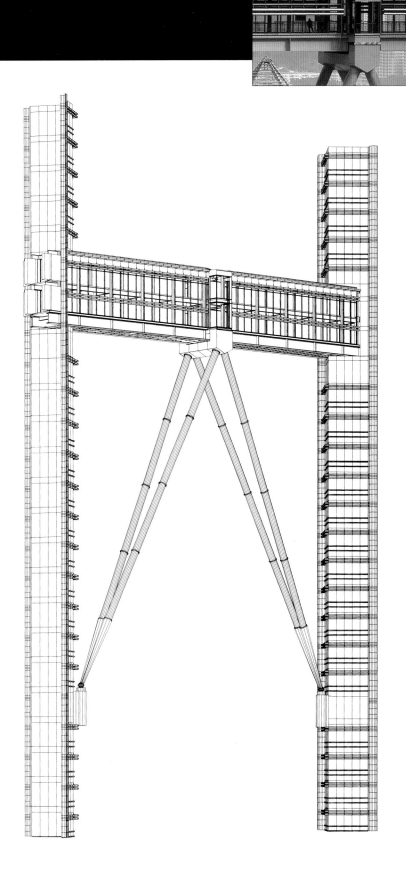

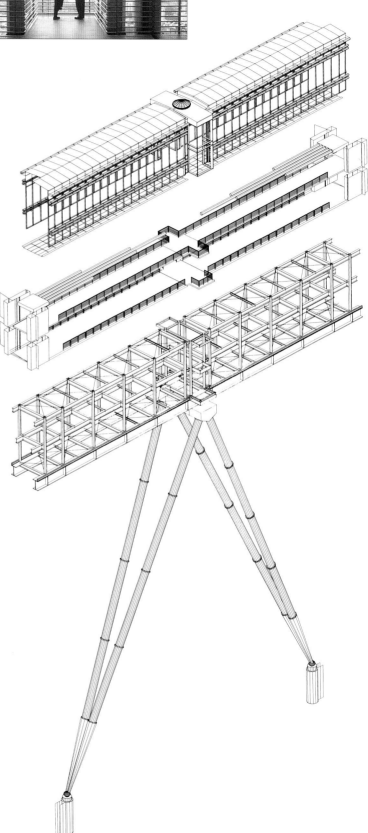

ABOVE LEFT: View through
upper level skybridge;
ABOVE RIGHT: View of
skybridge observation
area; RIGHT: Exploded
axonometric view of
skybridge;
OPPOSITE TOP: View of tower
curtainwall from skybridge;
OPPOSITE LEFT: View of
skybridge from adjacent
building; OPPOSITE RIGHT:
Frontal views of tower
tops, bustle tops
and skybridge

LEFT: View of towers' pinnacles looking east; OPPOSITE MIDDLE: Pinnacle curtainwall articulation studies; OPPOSITE LEFT: Model showing sloping pinnacle setbacks; OPPOSITE RIGHT: View up to tower pinnacles

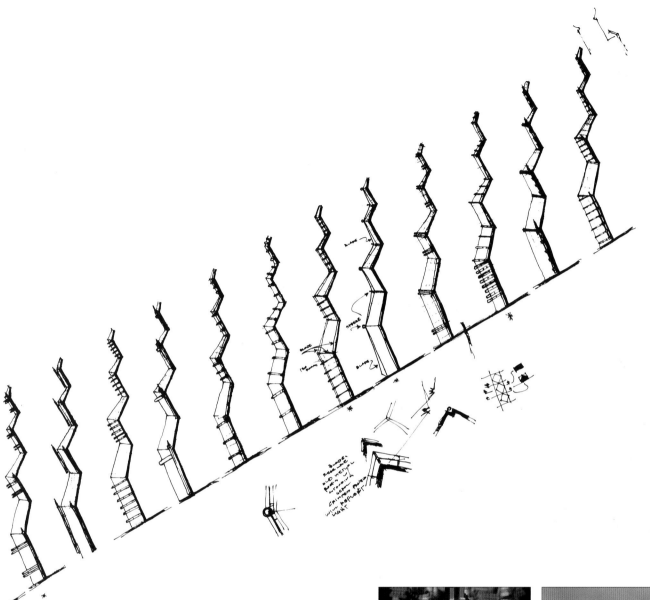

Petronas Towers

OPPOSITE LEFT: Perspective of tower pinnacle; OPPOSITE RIGHT: Interior view of pinnacle ring ball; BELOW: Curtainwall detail at level 88; RIGHT: View of tower one from tower two pinnacle base

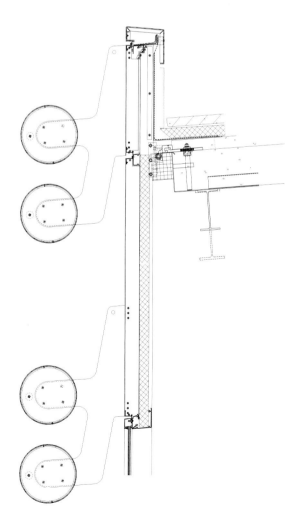

*ABOVE: Detail of the bustle
top of tower two, which
houses the Malaysian
Petroleum Club*

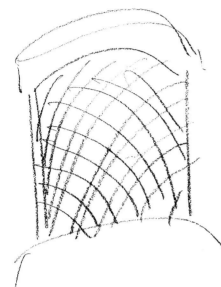

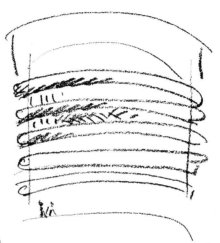

LEFT: View from street level of tower curtainwall; MIDDLE: Conceptual studies of bustle top; BELOW LEFT: Detail of tower two bustle curtainwall; BELOW RIGHT: Detail of tower one entrance

OPPOSITE LEFT: Detail of typical curtainwall at first tower set back; OPPOSITE RIGHT: Typical curtainwall with reflecting sunlight; ABOVE LEFT: Detail of curtainwall showing richness of stainless steel at sunset; ABOVE RIGHT: View up tower showing faceted curtainwall

ABOVE LEFT: Sectional view of tear-drop curtainwall sunshade during installation; RIGHT: Detail section of curtainwall at typical floor; OPPOSITE TOP: Conceptual sketch of curtainwall sunshade; OPPOSITE LEFT: View of curtainwall column cover; OPPOSITE RIGHT: Detailed view of faceted curtainwall showing projecting round and square bays

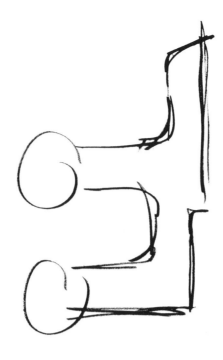

LEFT: Detail of stainless steel portico of tower entrance;
BELOW: Sunset view of entrance to towers and concert hall with Petronas Plaza in foreground

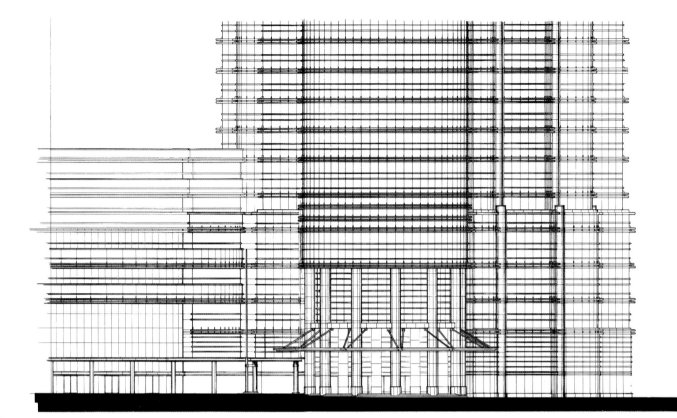

ABOVE: Elevation of tower
one entrance;
BELOW LEFT: Detail of
forecourt fountains
between tower entrances;
BELOW RIGHT: Forecourt
fountains

BELOW: Dusk view down allée of fountains of Petronas Plaza to concert hall entrance;
OPPOSITE LEFT: The drama of the concert hall entrance at night;
OPPOSITE RIGHT: View through lighted fountains of concert hall entrance and lobby; OPPOSITE BOTTOM: Axonometric of concert hall entrance

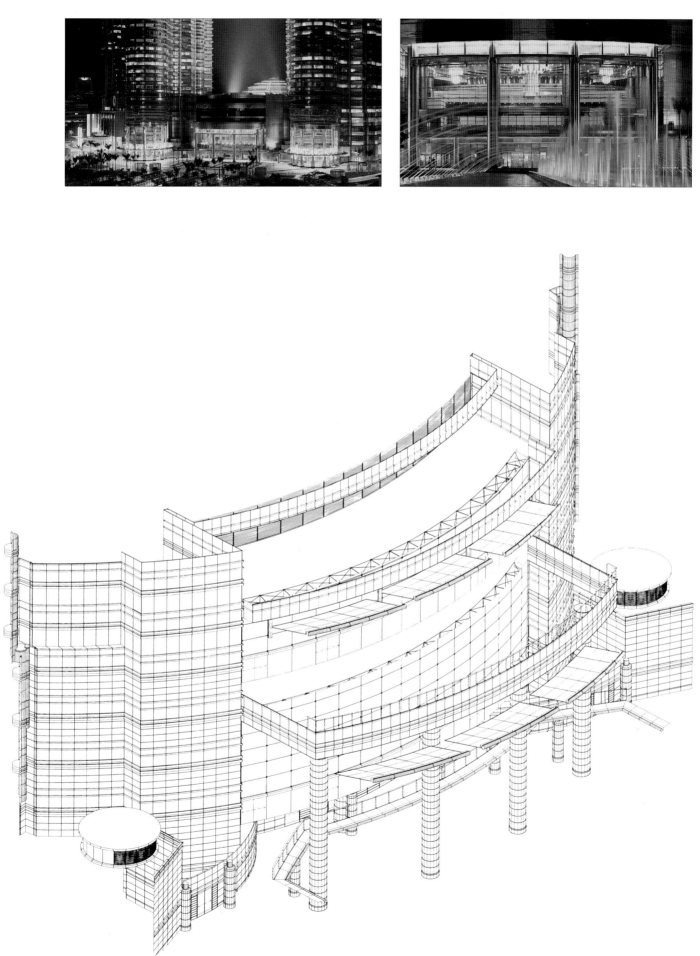

OPPOSITE: View of concert hall lobby prior to evening performance; ABOVE: Daytime view of concert hall lobby showing custom chandeliers, aluminum-leaf ceiling and Malaysian marble clad walls; BACKGROUND: Portico paving pattern; BELOW LEFT: View of custom stainless steel and glass chandelier from lobby; BELOW RIGHT: Detail of concert hall lobby floor showing radiating pattern of inlaid zinc and marble

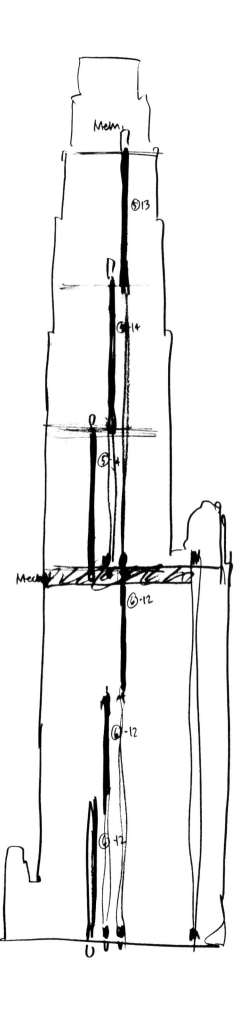

OPPOSITE TOP LEFT:
Conference center lobby at
level 40;
OPPOSITE BOTTOM:
Executive dining room;
OPPOSITE RIGHT:
Conceptual elevator
diagram; ABOVE:
Conference room at tower
one bustle top

ABOVE: View from rear of concert hall (Dewan Filharmonik Petronas); OPPOSITE LEFT: Orchestra level construction drawing of lobby and concert hall; OPPOSITE RIGHT: Detail of balconies' silicon bronze railings

PUBLIC REALM

The Dewan Filharmonik Petronas Concert Hall provides an important function in Pelli's design for Petronas Towers: a gathering space for the public to partake in civic celebration. This dovetails with the architect's conviction that the creation of such public, cultural spaces is a civic duty. Although this element of the towers' design was a late addition, it fits seamlessly with the overall goal of the structure to provide a place that is uniquely Malaysian.

One ascends to the concert hall from the lobby at the building's main entry. Grand staircases transport one up to the second level, where the 860-seat concert hall is situated. Inside, the soft warm tones of the wall finishes defer to a gleaming pipe organ at center stage. Under a dome and vaulted ceiling that are acoustically tuned, the hall can be modified to accommodate musical performances in both Eastern and Western traditions.

Another, larger dome is found in the a 1.5-million sq ft retail mall that hugs the base of Petronas Towers on its south side. The mall was designed by the Walker Group CNI, but the central dome is by Pelli. Appearing partially open, with sunlight glinting around its eight triangular sections, the dome defines the heart of this public arena. Each section steps up six times with clerestory windows to shed light on the underside of the dome's surface, and within its intricate structure.

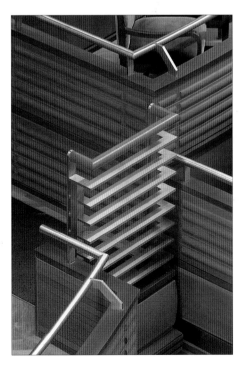

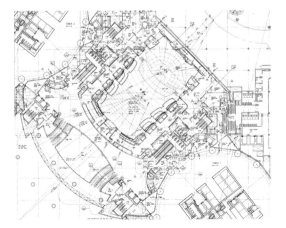

RIGHT: Elevation of rear
wall of concert hall with
VIP box in center;
BELOW LEFT: Detail of
custom-built, 44-stop
Klais organ;
BELOW RIGHT: Detail of
concert hall showing
acoustically articulated,
Malaysian-wood, box front;
OPPOSITE LEFT: View of
concert hall stage during
orchestral performance;
OPPOSITE RIGHT: View to
rear of concert hall prior
to performance;
OPPOSITE BOTTOM:
Longitudinal section
of concert hall

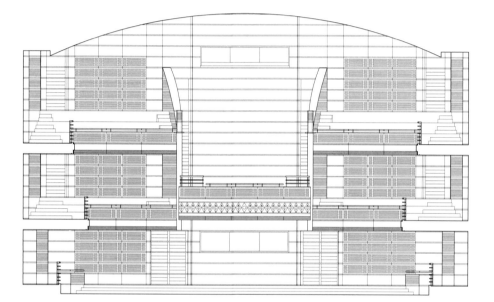

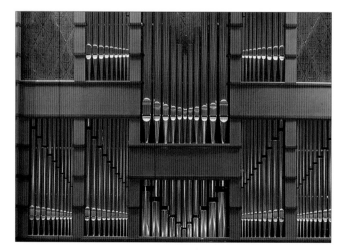

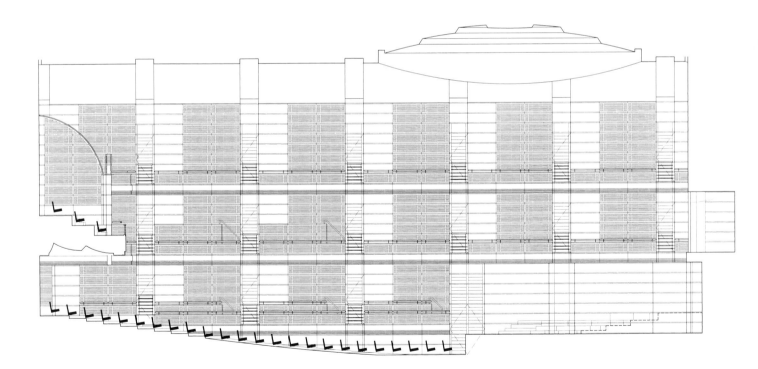

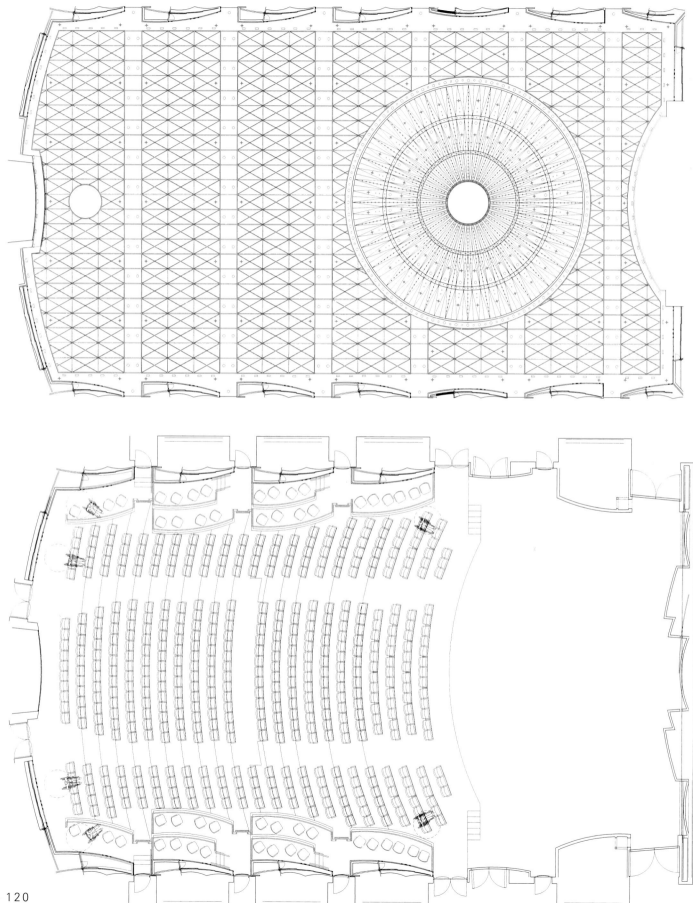

OPPOSITE TOP: Reflected
ceiling plan of concert hall;
OPPOSITE BOTTOM:
Orchestra level seating plan
of concert hall

ABOVE RIGHT: Detail of
concert hall chandelier and
fiber optic ceiling;
ABOVE LEFT: View up to
custom stainless steel and
art glass chandelier in
tower lobby;
RIGHT: Detail of concert
hall acoustic wood screens
and fiber optic ceiling

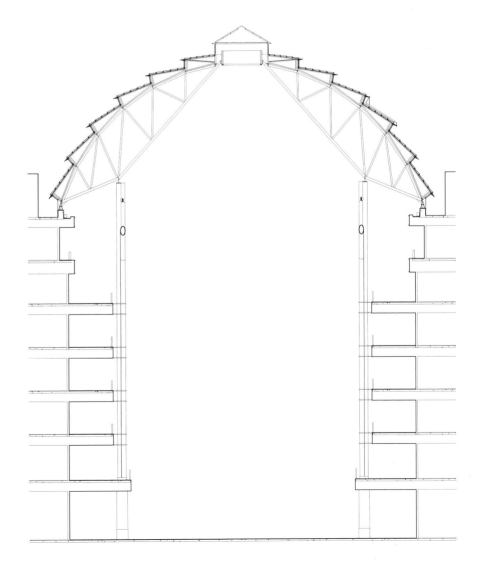

OPPOSITE TOP: View up to oval skylight atop the Suria KLCC retail court; OPPOSITE BOTTOM: View of retail court skylight and Roberto Burle Marx roofscape and park from skybridge; ABOVE: View up to oval skylight atop the Suria KLCC retail court; RIGHT: Cross section of Suria KLCC skylight and retail court

OPPOSITE: Dawn view of towers in city skyline with hills beyond;
RIGHT: Tower pinnacles silhouetted against the Kuala Lumpur sunrise

Petronas Towers Fact Sheet

Formal name of building	Petronas Towers
Location	Kuala Lumpur, Malaysia
Owner	Kuala Lumpur City Centre Holdings Sendirian Berhad
Architect	Cesar Pelli & Associates 1056 Chapel Street, New Haven, CT 06510 203.777.2515, Fax: 203.787.2856
Design Principal	Cesar Pelli FAIA
Project Principal and Collaborating Designer	Fred Clarke FAIA
Design Team Leader	Jon Pickard AIA
Project Manager	Larry Ng AIA
Designers	John Apicella, David Coon, Edward Dionne, Peter Follett, Michael Hilgeman, Russell Holcomb, Alison Horne, Gregg Jones, Vlad Simionescu, Heather Young, David Chen, John Clegg, Jerome del Fierro, Roberto Espejo, Sophie Harvey, Kristin Hawkins, Steven Marchetti, Robert Narracci, Dean Ober, Mark Outman, Enrique Pelli, Neil Prunier, Roger Schickedantz, BJ Siegel, David Strong, Jane Twombly
Architect of Record	KLCC Berhad Architectural Division, Kuala Lumpur, Malaysia
Associate Architect Landscape Design	Adamson Associates, Toronto, Ontario Balmori Associates, New Haven, CT NR Associates, Selangor, Malaysia
Structural Engineers	Thornton-Tomasetti Engineers, New York, NY; Ranhill Bersekutu Sdn. Bhd., Kuala Lumpur, Malaysia
MEP Engineers	Flack + Kurtz, New York, NY KTA Tenaga Sdn. Bhd., Kuala Lumpur, Malaysia

Consultants

Interior Designer	STUDIOS, San Francisco, California
Retail	Walker Group, CNI, New York, NY
Lighting	Howard Brandston & Partners, New York, NY
Curtain Wall	Israel Berger & Associates, New York, NY
Acoustical	Shen, Milsom & Wilke, Inc., New York, NY
Vertical Transportation	Katz Drago Company, Inc., Toronto, Ontario
Exterior Maintenance	Lerch Bates & Associates, Temecula, CA
Security	Techcord Consulting Group, Calgary, Alberta
Graphics	Emery Vincent, Melbourne, Australia
Life Safety	Rolf Jensen & Associates, Deerfield, IL
Traffic	Wilbur Smith Associates, Singapore
Parking	Central Parking Systems, Nashville, TN

Site/Civil	Ove Arup and Partners, Manchester, England Arup Jururunding, Kuala Lumpur, Malaysia
Wind Tunnel Testing	Rowan Williams Davies and Irwin (RWDI), Guelph, Ontario
General Contractor	Tower 1- Mayjus (Malaysia Japan Us) Joint-Venture MMC Engineering & Construction Co.Ltd. Ho Hup Construction Sdn. Bhd. Hazama Corporation/ JA Jones Construction Co. Ltd. Mitsubishi Corporation
	Tower 2- SKJ Joint-Venture Samsung Engineering & Construction Co. Ltd. Kuk Dong Engineering & Construction Co. Ltd. Syarikat Jasatera Sdn. Bhd.

Architectural Data

Height of the Towers	451.9 meters above street level (1,482.6 feet) 88 Occupiable Floors 4 below-grade levels
Height of Pinnacle	73.575 meters (241 feet)
Gross Building Area (each tower)	218,000 square meters / 2.3 million square feet
Size of Floor Plates (Gross)	Lower Floors: 2623.4 square meters / 28,239 square feet
Upper Floors	2089.3 square meters / 22,490 square feet to 929 square meters / 10,000 square feet
Typical Floor-to-Floor Height	4.0 meters / 13 feet, 2 inches
Finished Ceiling Height	2.65 meters/ 8 feet, 8 inches
Raised Floor	125mm (Floor 8 - Floor 72)
Skylobby	Levels 41 & 42 Amenities at Skylobby levels include conference centre, executive dining facilities and surau (prayer room.)

Skybridge		
Centre-line Span	58.44 meters
Overall Width	5.29 meters
Overall Height	9.45 meters
Length of Supports	51.50 meters
Total Weight	over 720 tonnes
# of pre-fab pieces	493

Main frame fabrication at SHI Chang Won #1 plant. Legs fabrication at SHI Koje Shipyard.

Exterior Cladding	Horizontal ribbons of vision glass and stainless steel spandrel panels. 85,000 square meters of cladding area above Level 6.

Foundation & Structure

Foundation   Two raft foundations 4.5m thick, each containing nearly 13,200 cubic meters of grade 60 concrete, which weighs approximately 32,350T; with 208 Barrette piles (rectangular section piles 2.8m x 1.2m), varying from 60 meters to 115 meters in length.

A perimeter diaphragm wall, 800mm thick.

Structure   A core and cylindrical tube frame system constructed entirely of cast-in-place high-strength concrete (up to Grade 80). Floor framing at tower levels are concrete fill of conventional strength on composite steel floor deck and composite rolled steel framing.

Vertical Transportation

Double-Deck and Skylobby Systems. Lower floors (Floors 8 - 37) are served by two banks of 6-1600/1600kg double-deck elevators. Upper floors (Floors 44 - 83) are served by one bank of 6-1600/1600kg, and two banks of 3-1600/1600kg double-deck elevators. Skylobbies (Floor 41 and 42) are served by five 2100/2100kg double-deck shuttle elevators.

Facts and Figures on Petronas Twin Towers from the Petronas web site

Number of Storeys	88
Overall Height	451.9m from street level
Height of Superstructure (without pinnacle)	378m
Tip of longest pile to tip of pinnacle mast	592.4m
Location of Skybridge	Levels 41 and 42
Length of Skybridge	58.4m
Height of Skybridge	170m from street level
Vertical Transportation	29 Double-deck high speed passenger lifts in each tower
Number of escalators	10 in each tower
Stainless Steel Cladding	65,000 sq m
Vision Glass	77,000 sq m
Concrete	160,000 cu m in the superstructure (various strength up to grade 80)
Steel	36,910 tonnes of beam, trusses and reinforcement
Foundation	4.5m (15 ft) thick raft containing 13,200 cu m of grade 60 concrete, weighing approximately 32,550 tonnes under each tower, supported by 104 barrette piles from 60m to 115m in length.

Dewan Filharmonik Petronas Fact Sheet

Client	Kuala Lumpur City Centre Berhad Petroliam Nasional Berhad
Design Consultant	Cesar Pelli & Associates, New Haven Connecticut
Design Principal	Cesar Pelli FAIA
Project Principal and Collaborating Designer	Fred Clarke FAIA
Design Team Leader	Jon Pickard AIA
Project Manager	Larry Ng AIA
Designers	John Apicella, J Bunton, David Coon, Edward Dionne, Peter Follett, Michael Hilgeman, Mitchell Hirsch, Russell Holcomb, Alison Horne, Keith Krolak, Dean Ober
Architect of Record	Architectural Division, Kuala Lumpur City Centre Berhad
Technical Consultant	Adamson Associates, Mississauga Ontario, Canada
Acoustic Consultant	Kirkegaard and Associates, Downers Grove, Illinois
Theater Design Consultant	Theatre Projects Consultants Inc., Ridgefield, Connecticut
Theater Operator	IMG Artists, London, England
Pipe Organ Fabricator	Orgelbau Klais Bonn, Bonn, Germany
Structural Engineer	Thorton-Tomasetti Engineers, New York, New York Ranhill Bersekutu Sdn. Bhd., Kuala Lumpur Malaysia
MEP Engineer	Flack+Kurtz, New York, New York KTA Tenaga Sdn. Bhd., Kuala Lumpur, Malaysia
Lighting Consultant	Howard Brandston & Partners, New York, New York
Construction Manager	Lehrer McGovern Malaysia, Kuala Lumpur, Malaysia
Theater Form	Shoebox
Seating Capacity	863
General Contractor	Comtrac Concrete Constructions JV Kuala Lumpur, Malaysia
	Concrete Constructions Group Australia
Design/Completion	1993/1998

Photographic credits

All photographs are courtesy of the architect unless stated otherwise; every effort has been made to locate sources and credit material but in the very few cases where this has not been possible our apologies are extended: Lee Dunnette p 16 (rendering), Kenneth M. Champlin pp 17, 20, 99 (left), Cesar Pelli & Associates p 23, J. Pickard/CP&A pp 30-41, 52, 53, 73, Rob Pritchett pp 42, 54, J. Apicella/CP&A pp 2, 43-47, 51 (bottom), 58-65, 71, 84, 91, 94 (middle and bottom), 97 (bottom right), 100-103, 107 (left), 109 (right), 110, 112, 122, D. Coon/CP&A pp 50, 51 (top), 56, Jeff Goldberg/Esto front cover, back cover, pp 66, 69, 72, 75-81, 85-89, 95 (top right), 96, 97 (top right and bottom left), 98, 99 (bottom right), 104-105, 107 (right), 108, 109 (left), 111, 113 (top and bottom left), 116-121, 123 (top right), 124, Photo courtesy Erco Licht p 67, 113 (bottom right), David Lok pp 82-83, L. Ng/CP&A pp 93, 94 (top), Peter Hyatt p 95 (bottom left), Jun Mitsui p 106, Michael O'Callahan pp 114-115, P. Follett/CP&A p 125.